Contents

Foreword   5

Introduction   7

Stage 1
Drawing and sign writing   11

Stage 2
Letter-like forms   19

Stage 3
Copied letters   27

Stage 4
Child's name and strings
of letters   35

Stage 5
Words   43

Stage 6
Sentences   51

Stage 7
Text   59

A bit of theory   69

Conclusion   71

References & further   72
reading

Assessing what children can do, in school and even before they start school, is a high priority for teachers at the moment. The development of early years education and the importance of learning in the early years make effective assessment important. Almost every parent is interested to know how their children's early skills develop and the stages they go through.

As part of the work we have been doing to develop family literacy programmes, Tom Gorman and Greg Brooks were asked to develop a framework to track the early writing development of young children from three to seven years old. This guide explains the seven stages of development which they identified based on more than 900 examples of children's writing. The guide also illustrates each stage.

Making a confident start in writing is important. I hope that the guide with its step by step approach helps those teaching children, or helping them at home, to track and support their development. As Greg and Tom point out, in the early stages it's as important to respond to children's interest and enthusiasm for writing as it is to teach them the formal elements of 'correct' writing.

I hope that both teachers and parents will find the guide practical and useful. It's not the only way of looking at early writing, but in our experience it works well. I would particularly like to thank Greg Brooks and Tom Gorman, as well as the families and teachers in the programmes, for the work which has gone into this guide.

Alan Wells OBE
Director
The Basic Skills Agency

Who is the guide for?

Assessing Young Children's Writing was developed by researchers, working with children, teachers and parents. It should be useful both to teachers working in Early Years and Primary education, and also to parents.

The guide identifies seven stages in the early development of children's writing. It could be used as part of Baseline Assessment and it should help you to:

- recognise the stage a child has reached
- anticipate what the next steps will be
- encourage children's development through them.

How was the guide developed?

From 1993 to 1995 the Basic Skills Agency supported four 'Family Literacy' programmes in Cardiff, Liverpool, Norfolk and North Tyneside. They worked with over 600 parents and young children between the ages of 3 and 7 (as well as younger children in crèches). One of the main aims of the programmes was to investigate and develop the many ways in which parents help their children to become confident readers and writers.

Because these were new pilot programmes there was also extensive research by a team from the National Foundation for Educational Research (NFER) led by Dr Greg Brooks. The researchers made over 20 visits to the programmes and gathered over 900 examples of the children's drawing and writing so that they could estimate their progress.

In order to identify and assess progress they had to devise a framework showing the different stages of development in the children's writing. This was done by Dr Tom Gorman who has more than thirty years' experience in the theory and practice of assessing writing. The teachers on the four programmes also had a major role, in working with the children who did the writing and in checking the developmental scale. There is a full report of the work of the programmes and NFER's evaluation of them in *Family Literacy Works* Basic Skills Agency 1996.

What were the children asked to do?

The teachers were given guidelines about what the children should be asked to do. Each example was to take one of the following forms:

- a few lines or a sentence if the child could do this;
- if not, then their own name and some other letters;
- if not that then a few attempts at letters, letter-like forms or scribbles;
- if not that then a copy of a few words;
- and if not that then a drawing.

The teachers were told that the main aim of the exercise was to produce the highest stage of writing that each child was capable of, **independently.** The range of examples listed above was therefore designed to cover the wide developmental range in 'writing' found among 3-7 year old children.

Examples were gathered near the beginning of the twelve week course and again at the end of the course. For some of the children there was a follow up nine months later when they were asked to give another example of their writing.

The seven stages

The starting points for the seven stage developmental scale were the examples the children produced and the researcher's knowledge of how these fitted with the usual stages of development. The examples move from what may look like scribbling (although children may already see it as marks which can give the reader a message) through to recognisable writing, which makes sense.

It's not the *only* way of looking at how writing develops, but in our experience it worked well across all the examples gathered and it did illustrate the key features of development. We therefore thought that it would be useful to produce a selection of the examples, and brief explanations, so that other people could use them.

When we look at how children learn to write we have to consider both how they learn to produce letters and words and also how they come to understand about using writing to convey meaning to the person reading. It's important not to concentrate just on the *form* of their first attempts to write, because from the beginning they are also involved in trying to communicate meaning.

In **Stage 1** *Drawing and sign writing* children are making shapes and lines on the page. For them these often have clear meanings, but the shapes do not look like letters. However, children at this stage often already understand that there is a difference between pictures and words.

In **Stages 2** *Letter-like forms*, **3** *Copied letters* and **4** *Child's name and strings of letters* they are learning the complicated business of how to form the shapes of individual letters. By the end of Stage 4 they are beginning to manage this on their own. The move from Stage 4 to Stage 5 Words is probably the most important of all. It is the 'taking off point' when children learn the fundamental idea of how to communicate meaning in writing.

In **Stages 5** *Words* and **6** *Sentences* they can begin to communicate ideas fluently. These are very important steps in the move towards being able to write on your own.

By **Stage 7** *Text* children can convey a set of related ideas in a way which makes sense. Once they have achieved Stage 5, many children can move on to Stages 6 and 7 quite quickly.

Ages and stages

We are used to the idea that when children learn to walk or talk their rate of progress varies. They may have spurts of progress and then seem to mark time for a while. Certainly it is difficult to generalise about the age at which they master different skills. In the same way there can be wide variation in the ages at which young children reach the different stages of writing, and the speed with which they move from one stage to the next.

As you can see from the examples, the ages of the children who produced them range from 3 years 10 months to 7 years 3 months. However, it's not a simple pattern in which all the early examples come from the youngest children. During the programmes some children moved very quickly through several stages. For example Rosheen wrote the example at Stage 5 (D); only twelve weeks later she was at Stage 7 (B). Other children progressed more steadily.

In our view it is not always useful to try and link the stages to ages in isolation. Writing is just one skill of many which children are learning and it's important to look also at how their talking and their reading are developing.

The National Curriculum

The early stages in the seven-point scale come, of course, well before the Levels set out in the National Curriculum and the descriptions of what children should learn to do in the early years of school. The Guidelines issued by the School Curriculum and Assessment Authority *Desirable Outcomes for Children's Learning* set out goals for children's achievements when they enter compulsory schooling. In writing, the goals are

'In their writing they use pictures, symbols, familiar words and letters, to communicate meaning, showing awareness of some of the different purposes of writing. They write their names with appropriate use of upper and lower case letters.'

By Stages 6 and 7 of the scale we move into an area which begins to overlap with the start of the National Curriculum. To achieve Level 1 of the National Curriculum in writing what children should be able to do is described like this:

'Pupils' writing communicates meaning through simple words and phrases. In their reading or their writing pupils begin to show awareness of how full stops are used. Letters are usually clearly shaped and correctly orientated.'

For Level 2 the description is:

'Pupils' writing communicates meaning in both narrative and non-narrative forms, using appropriate and interesting vocabulary, and showing some awareness of the reader. Ideas are developed, in a sequence of sentences, sometimes demarcated by capital letters and full stops. Simple, monosyllabic words are usually spelt correctly and where there are inaccuracies the alternatives are usually phonetically plausible. In handwriting, letters are accurately formed and usually consistent in size.'

All the children whose writing is shown in this booklet, up to Stage 6, are *working towards* Level 1 of the National Curriculum. By Stage 6 they are using simple phrases, even sentences, but they show little awareness of how full stops are used and their handwriting still varies in its shape and direction.

Some of the children at Stage 7 are working within Level 1, and the final example shows a child working within Level 2. It's important to remember that in the family literacy research just one example of a child's writing was considered at each assessment. For the National Curriculum a teacher takes account of many examples, across a range of different writing, by each child. Of course a child whose writing is shown here might, later in the year, have moved from one level to another.

The examples
The examples of children's writing have been reduced to approximately half their original size.

Drawing and sign writing

Children were asked to draw a person. The first two examples show what they did.

At an early stage children do a kind of sign writing, with their pictures. This is an early form of writing. While it might look like scribbling to us, children often think of it as writing. They are already getting an idea about how writing works, and understanding that we use marks on the page to pass ideas from the writer to the reader.

In the examples the words have been written by the teachers, when the children explained their drawings.

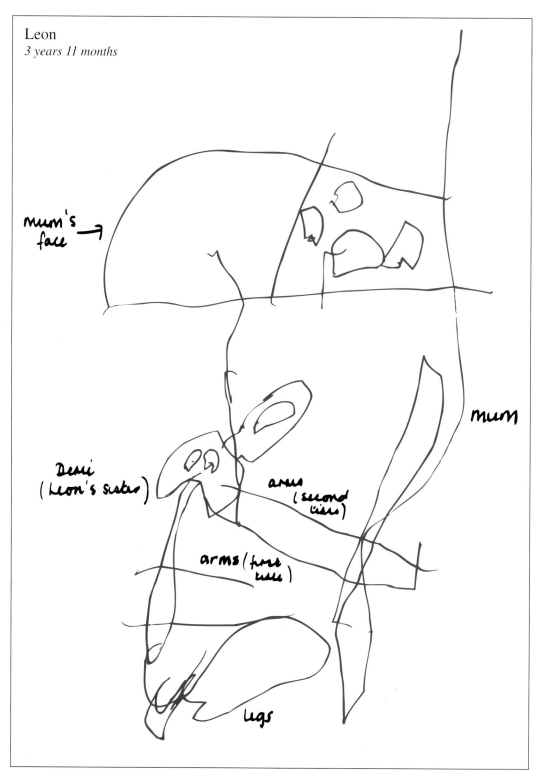

Leon
3 years 11 months

mum's face →

mum

Desu (Leon's sister)

arms (second ones)

arms (first ones)

legs

Example A

At first sight we might not be able to understand this picture. The labels have been added by the teacher and they show that Leon has a clear idea about what each part of the drawing means.

Jessica
4 years 3 months

Example B

In this picture Jessica has put eyes, nose and lips on her person, and she has drawn the right number of arms and legs.

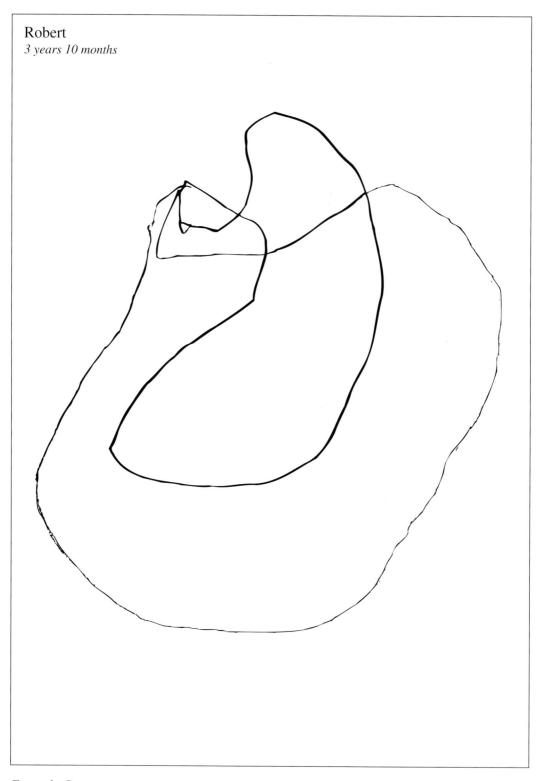

Robert
3 years 10 months

Example C
We know from the teacher that this is Robert's first try at 'writing'.

Nathan
4 years 3 months

Example D

In this example we can see that Nathan can use his hand to control the pencil and the shapes he makes, which is important before you begin to form the shapes of letters. Some of his shapes are like the patterns of writing.

Daniel
3 years 10 months

Example E

To make these shapes Daniel had to use the same kind of control over his pencils that you need to form letters.

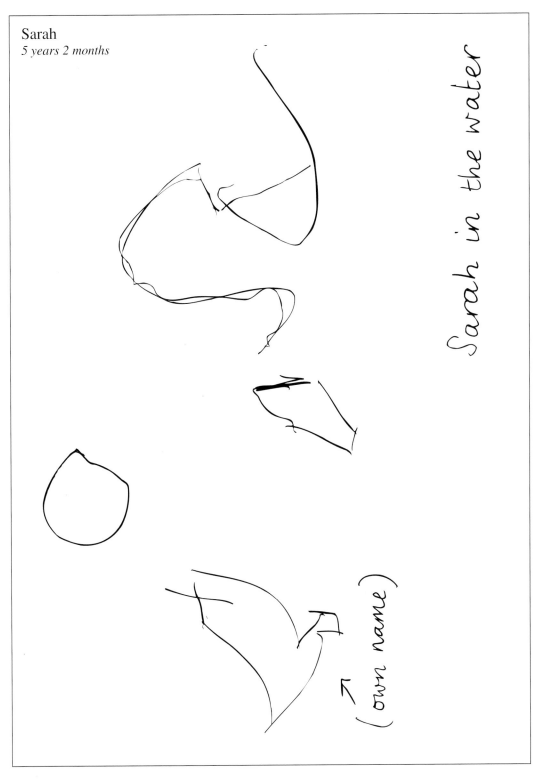

Sarah
5 years 2 months

Sarah in the water

(own name)

Example F

Sarah has made one set of shapes for her own name and another for the picture of her in the water. Even though we might not be able to recognise the shapes, this shows that she is getting the idea of pictures and words as two separate things.

Letter-like forms

Learning to write letters correctly involves very careful observation and advanced hand control and coordination. Children see many different types and sizes of script around them every day; so learning to use the particular forms used by their teachers requires a lot of practice.

4 years 2 months

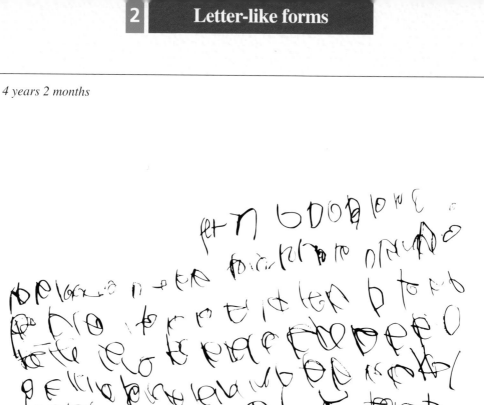

Example A

This is an example where the child is moving on from stage 1. She cannot write letters yet, but she knows some important things about writing. She knows that it goes in lines, from left to right, and from the top of the page to the bottom.

Charlotte
4 years 11 months

Example B

Charlotte knows the difference between pictures and words. The forms she uses are beginning to look like letters in her own name, which we can recognise. She has not learned yet about writing from left to right.

Daniel
5 years 2 months

Example C

Daniel has written his idea of the first letters of his name. Often the letters in their name are the first ones children try to write. We can see that Daniel has used some of the shapes which are in the letters of the alphabet.

Ben
4 years 2 months

Example D

Ben is getting close to the shapes of the letters in his name, and we can recognise them when we see them next to the teacher's wrting.

Kristie
4 years 2 months

Example E

Kristie is writing under and over letters written by the teacher. We can see that this is helping her to have some control over the shapes she makes.

India
5 years 2 months

Example F

India is moving on to the next stage. We can almost recognise the letters, which she has copied.

Copied letters

Stages 2 and 3 are very close to one another. In Stage 3 children can form letters, if they have help. This may be letters to write *over*, letters to write *under*, or letters to *copy*.

Kirsty
4 years 9 months

Example A

When she writes over the teacher's letters, Kirsty can manage to make the shapes of letters quite accurately. She has also tried to write the letters underneath. We can recognise some of the letters, for example 'T', 'm', 'B', 'w', 's'. Sometimes they are turned around (reversed), and many letters are written on a slant.

Christopher
4 years 11 months

Christopher

Chsopne

Example B

Writing over the teacher's letters, Christopher can control the shapes of the letters quite well.
We can recognise some of the letters he has written by himself, underneath.

Stephen
4 years 4 months

Example C

In the same way, Stephen has managed to make letters, over the dots the teacher has given, and underneath he has started to make letter shapes of his own.

Craig
5 years 9 months

craig

The bikes go fast.

Thebikesgofast

Example D

Craig can write most of the letters so that we can recognise them. So far he does not know about spaces between words, or writing straight across the page.

Laura
5 years 0 months

Example E

In the writing Laura has done, underneath the teacher's, all the letters and words can be read.

6 years 4 months

Example F

This child has copied from another piece of paper, which is more difficult than writing over or under the teacher's writing. All the letters and words can be recognised, even though they are not written in straight lines.

Child's name and strings of letters

In stage 4, and all the ones which follow, children are writing on their own, **independently**, without copying over the teacher's writing.

Once children can write different letters of the alphabet they very often start by using these to write their own name. This does not mean that they understand, yet, how letters can be combined to convey the sounds of their names.

Samantha
5 years 7 months

Samantha wrote her Christian name without help. She then wrote individual letters which she thought were words, wrote curly 'c' and 'o' and then drew herself, and below, her Dad.

Example A

We can see from the teacher's comment that Samantha wrote her own name by herself. Then she wrote some letters she knows – which she thought of as words.

Corrin
4 years 0 months

Example B

Corrin can also write his own name by himself. Next he has written a line of letters which he knows how to write.

Craig
4 years 10 months

Example C

Craig can write his name by himself. On his picture he has written lines of letters, all of which we can recognise. He does not yet know how to combine letters into words. He said that what he had written was: 'Me and my dad are doing the car'.

John
6 years 2 months

Example D

John's writing is at the same stage of development as Craig's. We can see that he can control the shapes of the letters well.

6 years 1 month

Example E

This child wanted to write: 'The bear was going to sleep in the car but the sun came up'. So he has got the idea of putting a message across through writing and making a sentence which tells us what is happening in a picture. He does not yet know about writing each word separately.

5 years 9 months

Example F

This child is moving on to the next stage. She has got the idea of forming separate words with groups of letters. But we cannot read what she has written ('Mr Bear went to the car and he fell asleep') because the letter strings are not yet close enough to the spelling of the words she wants to write.

Words

When children reach stage 5 they have crossed the **threshold to literacy**. They have learnt to associate the sounds of groups of letters with words in the spoken language. They are now able to express concepts in writing.

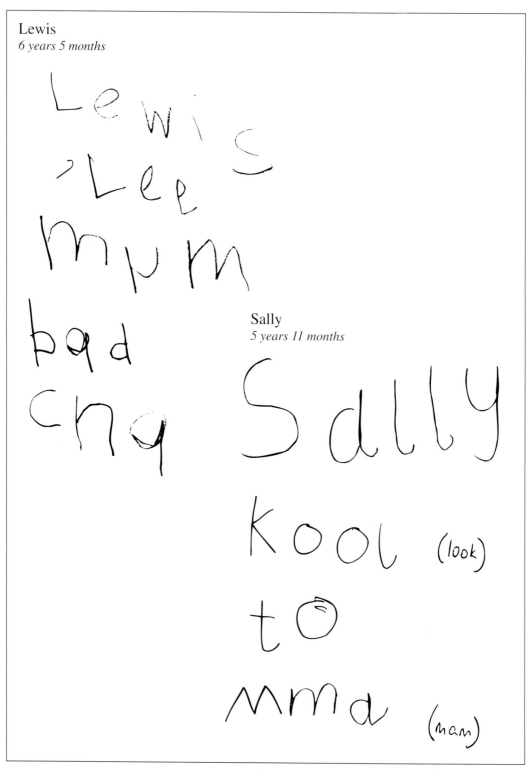

Lewis
6 years 5 months

Sally
5 years 11 months

Example A

Lewis and Sally both understand that you use strings of letters to write words. In both of their lists, some letters are reversed and sometimes the letters are in the wrong order.

J.J.
6 years 1 month

Example B

Children often see words used to label things. In this picture JJ has written words to label parts of the drawing.

Nadine
5 years 10 months

Example C

Nadine has also used words to label her drawing. She understands about dividing words.

Rosheen
6 years 4 months

Ro s he e n Cat and dog

Example D
We can read the words in this piece, even though they are not yet written as separate units.

Anthony
5 years 3 months

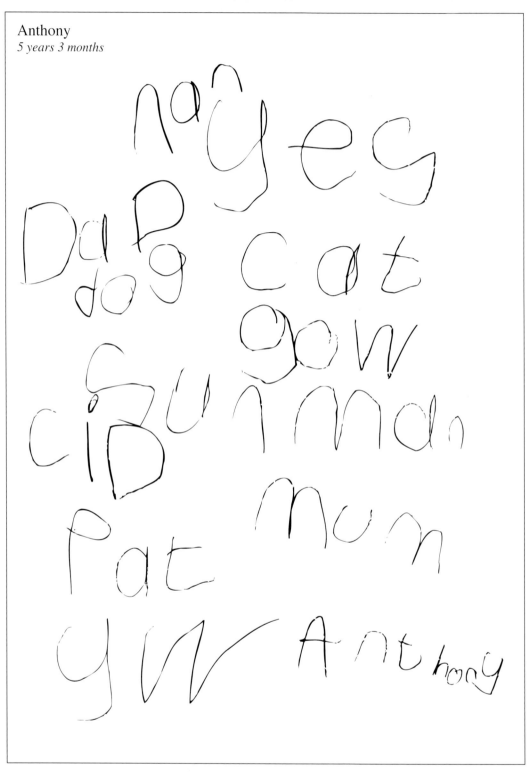

Example E

Anthony has written a list of words he knows. It is likely that these are words he has learned to read and write as whole words.

Robert
5 years 4 months

Robert   LOOK

can in
cant   is

My   mum is doing
My   mum is doing

the dishes
the dishes

Example F

Robert can write whole words, which he can also read. Writing under the teacher's writing, he has separated the words. So he could probably move to the next stage of writing sentences by himself.

Sentences

Once children have learnt to write separate words they can begin to put ideas into writing. To do this they need to use sentences.

6 years 2 months

I m⌀ boy

Wrote "I am a boy" independently

Example A

The most simple sentences tell the reader a fact, or an opinion. We can read this child's statement 'I am a boy' even though he is not yet quite sure about dividing words and leaving spaces between them.

Lindsay
6 years 8 months

I LiKe chips

Lindsay

Jôn-Paul
5 years 10 months

JÔh-PauL EScott

I like my Seuf

I like myself

Example B

These are sentences which the children wrote in booklets about themselves. In the second one the child is more certain about leaving spaces between words.

steven

a big
ber
is
hibin
bhid
a
tres.

Steven
4 years 4 months

Example C

Steven is writing a description, as part of telling a story. He has not written in lines across the page, but the way he writes fits with his picture.

Example D

We can understand the description in this writing even though the letter *s* is always written backwards. Alysiyia has a good idea of spacing her words and she also shows that she has some idea about separating sentences by starting a new line for 'My sister is on the swing'.

6 years 2 months

weⁿT woz a babey
Tcoduⁿotswim.

Example E

This is the first example where we see a full stop at the end of the sentence. Although the examples in Stage 6 show children beginning to write sentences, they do not generally use full stops or capital letters.

Shakira
6 years 4 months

Shakira

Shakira wrote most of this by herself; I helped tell her how to spell 'three' and 'house' - the rest she worked out for herself.

The Three bears
house oandyy Dadbear
Sed to by by beorahd
mumbearltisahisdyy
for poruris

Example F

Shakira is moving on to the next stage. She has given a title, although it is not clearly separated from the first sentence. Her writing is nearly at the stage we could call a piece of *text*.

Text

In this study, pieces of writing that contained three or more clauses were classified as **texts**, provided that they also shared other characteristics of texts. The most important characteristics are that they are coherent in **meaning** and **structure**.

In meaning, a text conveys a sequence of related ideas. In structure, a writer uses different ways to link what is being written with what went before, and what follows, so that the whole piece holds together. The links can be in the grammar and in the use of words.

Children often write quite long and complex sentences, using different ways of linking the separate parts. For example, there are nine clauses in the sentence in example G.

Often the ideas in a text are presented in a way that differs according to the type of text being written. As well as learning about sentence structure, children also learn how to construct stories and other types of text, such as explanations and descriptions.

6 years 3 months

I went to the caravan to clean it out Then I went to play football

This was written independently. Help was given with spelling the underlined words.

Example A

This is the simplest type of text. It gives a short account of personal experience. The two sentences, linked by 'then', are made up of two finite verb phrases and one non-finite verb phrase ('to clean it out').

Rosheen
6 years 7 months

RoSheen Flynn.
BeRNadeTTeFlynn.
william Flynn.
dugey creen.
I have A a cat.
it Sat on the mat
It have got A hamse.
it runs A rand.
I have A frendsee
Redece is my frend.

Example B

This example also has a very simple text structure. It is a list of 'possessions', each one named in a sentence, set out on a single line. This structure reflects the child's lack of experience in writing text. The use of line breaks to separate sentences does however help the child to present her ideas clearly. It is often used by children who are learning to write texts.

6 years 0 months

I went to the park and played on the saly and played On the swings and the minkiy bonys

Example C

This script does not make use of spaces to divide words and this makes the writing more difficult to read. Most children go through this stage in their writing. It is interesting to note that in the development of writing, for example in Latin and Greek, divisions between words and sentences came at quite a late stage.

Kerrie
6 years 9 months

KerrieBurrows
i tis Easrr sown Lost Eastr I wenc
on holaday toslow Forlodays
I om gowingto tunisa on the 11of
Joun my mum Looks after my gran
and grandads house my Birthday
is the 8of Joun I will die>

Example D

This script also shows that Kerrie is not yet experienced in getting meaning across to the
reader or in structuring the writing. So far as the meaning is concerned, we cannot see at once
the connections between the different subjects (the date of her birthday and the fact that her
mum looks after her Gran's house) although there may be links between these and the theme
of Easter and holidays. So far as structure is concerned the child does not use spacing or
punctuation to separate sentences and this makes it harder to read what she has written, but it
is still possible to understand it.

6 years 4 months

my Shists had a Patiy and we.playd
mykuicis. and we had a basiykasuL.and. We
pLayd statys. aad the basiykasuLmen
cam to tak tikit a way●

Example E

This child has been very ingenious in trying to spell 'sisters', 'musical chairs', 'bouncy castle', and 'take it away', by getting as close as she can to the sounds of the words. Her attempts at doing this (and the fact that she puts a full stop each time she uses the word 'and') make it difficult, but not impossible, to understand the writing.

4 years 7 months

I went to my
nans to have a
rosd dinner and
after we had
a rest we ate
some ais-creem
and it was
yellow and brown
and pink

and I went to the beach with
zoo and the mums and me
Crisdel and kenny went and the end and
the water and we got some Sunbirnt
on hor back and we saw a
Gelie fish and it bite crisdel

Example F

As well as linking sentences with 'and' this child also makes use of subordination in saying
when she ate the multi-coloured ice cream. The shape of the text reminds us that children also
have to learn how to set out a text on the page.

6 years 6 months

I went to the Satdey CLub and on Sunday We went to guLivewild and Me and Ben and Jennerer Went on the cup's and Suses two time's and then we Went on Ladiy Bird and then we went to haev Lunce and we woted a Shoe and the next day I went to ScoLeL and I CuLid in and then I dun gum ratin.

Example G

This sentence-paragraph of nine clauses, ending with a full stop, is typical of the way that children who are learning to write tend to use full stops to separate sections of a text (paragraphs rather than sentences). Janet White has shown that this tendency reflects the child's knowledge of spoken language.

Sally

6 years 1 month

This is a christmas story
christmas is special
because Jesus was born on
the first christmas mary ll looked after
Jesus because He was special.

Sally had help writing the long words, but can write the keywords independently.

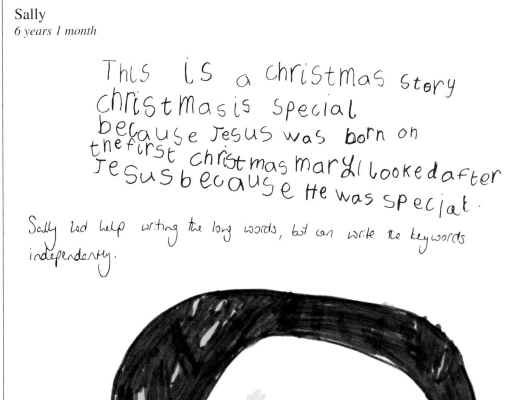

Example H

This example of writing presents Sally's view of why Christmas is 'special'. It begins with a statement, distinct from the rest of the account, indicating that it is a Christmas story. In this simple respect, as well as in the way it repeats subordinate clauses, this piece of writing is a more 'developed' text than the earlier ones.

7 years 3 months

Once a poyne time ther was to twins ther
names wer Cisdy a Clowy. Thay a was Played to
geather. One day ther mym and dad tyrk ther
them to the fer. thay went on the Little
boby horses. Thay time wer frintca of the
rids. Then it was to go home. wen the big
got home Thay went up Stirs to play with
ther toys.

Example I

This final example of children's writing is taken from the scripts assembled in the nine-month follow-up study. At this stage many of the children were capable of independent writing. The script shows a number of characteristics associated with writing at Level 2 in the National Curriculum for English (outlined on page 9). The writing shows some awareness of the reader in the way the simple narrative is introduced and in the logical structure of the account. The sentences in the account are linked in a time sequence.

We did not think that it was appropriate to present a detailed discussion in this booklet of the theories that underlie the method of classifying children's writing, but it seems relevant to say a little more about this. The following chart summarises the main components of the system of classification used. There are three sections in the left hand column. These show the different types of meaning, or ways meaning is organised, which children have to master. The two middle columns show formal elements. These are the features of written language which children need to learn in order to get their meaning on to paper. In the right-hand column are the seven stages set out in this guide.

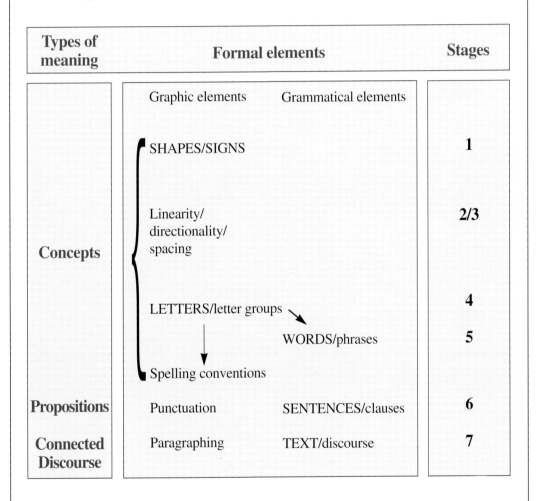

Types of meaning	Formal elements		Stages
	Graphic elements	Grammatical elements	
	SHAPES/SIGNS		1
	Linearity/ directionality/ spacing		2/3
Concepts	LETTERS/letter groups		4
		WORDS/phrases	5
	Spelling conventions		
Propositions	Punctuation	SENTENCES/clauses	6
Connected Discourse	Paragraphing	TEXT/discourse	7

This chart illustrates that, in learning to write, a child first learns to distinguish between drawing and writing, between shapes and signs. Children learn that writing is written in lines from left to right (linearity and directionality). They gradually learn to distinguish the many different shapes that make up the letters of the alphabet and at the same time to associate different letters with different sounds and names. They become familiar with particular groups of letters separated by spaces from other groups. The breakthrough to literacy comes when the child personally learns to associate the sounds of these groups of letters with words or names they already use in speech. After that stage, the transition to reading and writing groups of words in sentences and texts follows quickly.

It is obvious that, as soon as children begin to put marks on paper, they are intent on communicating meaning. To begin with, the fact they they do not yet know the graphic elements of writing stands in the way of writing a connected text, but, from the start, that is what they are trying to do.

Our examination of children's writing has shown that the development of grammatical punctuation, including the systematic use of full stops and of a capital letter to start a sentence, is something that usually occurs *after* children have begun to write texts fluently. Mastery of other aspects of the writing system, such as the systematic distinction between upper and lower case letters and knowledge of the principles of English spelling, also develops or continues to develop *after* children have learnt to produce coherent texts.

It takes several years to learn all the different codes used in writing, particularly the conventions of spelling, so it is wrong to discourage children from producing texts until they can transcribe them accurately. Nor is it helpful to overemphasise the need for accurate spelling at too early a stage of development. An overemphasis on punctuation and spelling at too early a stage quickly leads children to dislike writing and to avoid it where possible.

Parents and teachers therefore need to be alert to signs that children are developing in their ability to produce texts as soon as they begin to write sentences. Katharine Perera, an authority on children's writing, made a similar point when she wrote that 'instances of constructions that show a sensitivity to discourse structure . . . may gleam through a piece that is badly written, poorly punctuated and atrociously spelt – and provide encouraging evidence that something is being learnt'. She has shown that some of the grammatical developments of writing – *which are different from those of speech in several ways* – seem to arise from the need to structure text coherently. This points to 'the importance of encouraging children to write continuous prose from an early age'.

If the children whose work is shown in this guide, and other children of their age, are to continue developing as fluent writers they will need encouragement to:

- **read a wide range of stories and information books**

- **hear an even wider range of books read to them**

- **write texts for different purposes**

- **get balanced advice from parents and teachers about the content, organisation, and style of what they write, and its accuracy.**

Brooks, G., Gorman, T., Harman, J., Hutchison, D., Wilkin, A., *Family Literacy Works* The Basic Skills Agency 1996.

Clay, M., *Writing begins at home* Heinemann 1987.

Consistency in Teacher Assessment Exemplification of Standards: English Key Stages 1 & 2, Levels 1 to 5 Reading, Writing SCAA 1995.

Czerniewska, P., *Learning about writing* Blackwell 1992.

Nursery Education Desirable Outcomes for Children's Learning on entering compulsory education SCAA 1996.

Perera, K., 'Grammatical differentiation between speech and writing in children aged 8 to 12' in Carter R. (ed), 1990 *Knowledge about Language and the Curriculum: the LINC Reader* London Hodder and Stoughton, pp.218-233.

White, J. 'Children's Writing at Age 7', Appendix 4 in Cato V, Gorman T, and Kispal A, *The Teaching of Initial Literacy: How do teachers do it?* Slough: NFER p.56, 1992.